owep

AUG 2009

D1191058

Learn With Animals/
Aprende con los animales

Animal Opposites/
Opuestos animales

Sebastiano Ranchetti

Reading consultant: Susan Nations, M.Ed.,
author/literacy coach/consultant
in literacy development/

Consultora de lectura: Susan Nations, M.Ed.,
autora/tutora de lectoescritura/
consultora de desarrollo de lectoescritura

WEEKLY READER®
PUBLISHING

2

big
----
grande

small
----
pequeño

3

4

- - - - -
alto

low
- - - - - -
bajo

5

long
----
largo

short
- - - - - -
corto

up

- - - - - - - -

arriba

down

- - - - - - - -

abajo

8

9

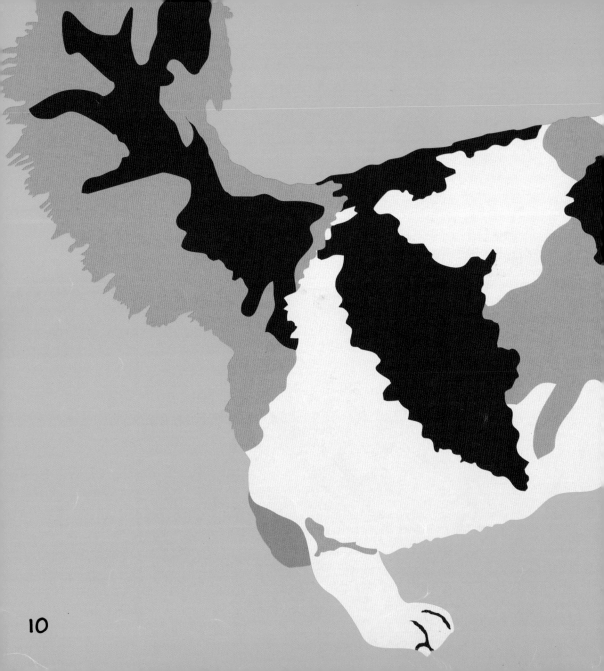

soft
- - - - - - - - -
suave

hard
- - - - - - - -
duro

11

light
------
claro

dark
----
oscuro

morning
----
mañana

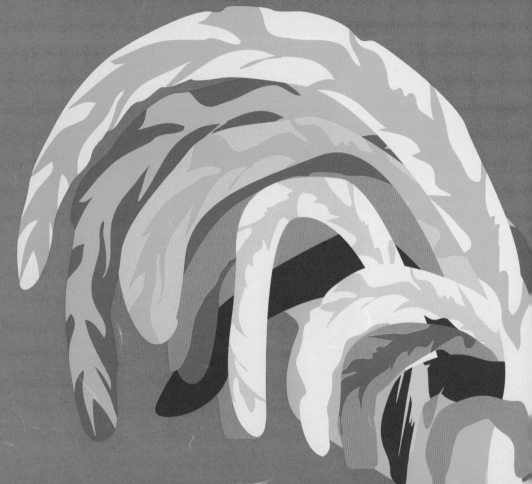

night

----

noche

15

slow
----
lento

fast

----

rápido

17

less

- - - - - - - -

menos

more
------
más

alone

------

solo

together
----
juntos

big
----
grande

small
----
pequeñ

high
----
alto

low
----
bajo

long
----
largo

short
----
corto

up
----
arriba

down
----
abajo

soft
----
suave

hard
----
duro

22

light
-----
claro

dark
----
oscuro

morning
----
mañana

night
----
noche

slow
-----
lento

fast
-----
rápido

less
----
menos

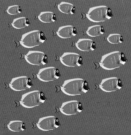

more
----
más

Please visit our web site at www.garethstevens.com.
For a free color catalog describing our list of high-quality books,
call 1-800-542-2595 (USA) or 1-800-387-3178 (Canada). Our fax: 877-542-2596

Library of Congress Cataloging-in-Publication Data available upon request from publisher.

ISBN-10: 0-8368-9038-8   ISBN-13: 978-0-8368-9038-9 (lib. bdg. : alk. paper)
ISBN-10: 0-8368-9043-4   ISBN-13: 978-0-8368-9043-3 (softcover)

This North American edition first published in 2008 by
Weekly Reader® Books
An Imprint of Gareth Stevens Publishing
1 Reader's Digest Road
Pleasantville, NY 10570-7000   USA

This North American edition first published in 2008 by
Weekly Reader® Books
An Imprint of Gareth Stevens Publishing
1 Reader's Digest Road
Pleasantville, NY 10570-7000   USA

Gareth Stevens Senior Managing Editor: Lisa M. Guidone
Gareth Stevens Senior Editor: Barbara Bakowski
Gareth Stevens Creative Director: Lisa Donovan
Gareth Stevens Graphic Designer: Alexandria Davis
Spanish Translators: Tatiana Acosta and Guillermo Gutiérrez

About the AUTHOR and ARTIST
SEBASTIANO RANCHETTI has illustrated many books. He lives in the countryside near Florence, Italy. His wife, three daughters, and some lively cats and dogs share his home. The ideas for his colorful drawings come from nature and animals. He hopes his books spark your imagination! Find out more at **www.animalsincolor.com**.

Información sobre el AUTOR/ARTISTA
SEBASTIANO RANCHETTI ha ilustrado muchos libros. Vive en el campo cerca de Florencia, Italia, con su esposa, sus tres hijas y algunos traviesos gatos y perros. Sebastiano se inspira en la naturaleza y los animales para sus coloridos dibujos, y espera que sus libros estimulen tu imaginación. Para más información, visita **www.animalsincolor.com**.